EMBERLYN ASHEN

FROM ASPIRATIONS TO ACHIEVEMENT

Nurturing Your Millionaire Mindset

This book was professionally typeset on Reedsy.
Find out more at reedsy.com

Contents

1

INTRODUCTION

We all have a similar thread in the vast fabric of life: the desire to pursue our goals and the hope of a better, more affluent future. Each of us has a deep-seated yearning for financial stability and the freedom to live our lives as we want. But far too frequently, this goal seems like a dazzling mirage that is always just out of grasp.

Here you will find information about "From Aspirations to Achievement: Nurturing Your Millionaire Mindset." This book is neither a guarantee of overnight success or a guide to fast money. Instead, it serves as a guide—a dependable travel partner—along your path to financial plenty and personal development.

On a journey that goes beyond the idea of just gaining riches, we shall set out in these pages. The depth of your fulfillment and the richness of your life experiences are the true measures of prosperity in this context rather than only financial gain.

Many people now see the "millionaire mindset" as a seductive sign of possibility. To be clear, though, there is neither a miraculous wand nor a quick route to inexhaustible wealth. It takes commitment, understanding, and the development of particular habits to succeed financially. At the same time, you must remain anchored in the realization that genuine prosperity is more than just financial achievement.

Our goal in writing these pages is to provide you the knowledge and understanding necessary to cultivate a mentality that will lead to possibilities, open doors, and financial independence. The principles of financial literacy, the practice of ethical investment, and the possibilities of entrepreneurship will all be covered. We will also examine the psychological and emotional aspects of wealth since your connection with money is just as crucial as your capacity for earning it.

Keep in mind that you are the one who holds the compass that directs your destiny as we set out on this trip together. "From Aspirations to Achievement" is your go-to road map, providing insight, tips, and helpful guidance to help you negotiate the sometimes challenging terrain of career advancement and personal improvement.

So flip the page and let's start our trip if you're ready to cultivate your millionaire mindset, adopt the principles of success, and open the door to your financial ambitions. Your ambitions are the seeds of your success, and with the appropriate mentality, they have the potential to grow beyond your greatest dreams.

2

INTRODUCTION TO THE MILLIONAIRE MINDSET

I t takes effort to enter. It shapes your routines, work style, and personal as well as professional behavior. Let's briefly go through what that attitude entails. It entails letting go of undesirable, harmful, and mind-numbing traits while also fostering the development of discipline, attention, good health, and creativity. When you put in the effort to develop your strategic thinking skills, it affects every aspect of your life. You form the habits of creating objectives, considering how to reach those goals, and assigning yourself deadlines; you then put in a lot of effort, study hard, and allow your imagination guide you.

Spending time doing things you don't naturally do is a significant component of the millionaire mindset. You may take up learning an instrument, picking up chess, joining a bridge group, learning to sew, or taking yoga lessons. Exercising your comfort zone can make you more at ease in both your professional and personal life. Your actions will gradually reflect all of the different traits you are acquiring. You'll develop into a more engaging someone who makes better friends and whom others love being around.

You'll notice in your personal life that the individuals you hang out with either support the new you or wander away. That's all right. When you are surrounded by people who frequently waste time and energy, it can be challenging to develop solid life skills. People who are intelligent, hardworking, and aware that life is about much more than just making money will be drawn to you. Even if your initial motivation for wanting to become a billionaire may have been the ability to buy everything you wanted, you will discover that by the time you had one million dollars in the bank, you have changed. You will have changed for the better and will be a new person if you did a decent job in the beginning of this process.

Understanding wealth mindset

Knowing the wealth mentality is like seeing into the machine that makes money. It's not only about gaining money; it's about reprogramming your mind to think prosperously. This way of thinking recognizes that the notion of wealth has many facets, including not only material prosperity but also personal fulfillment, a feeling of purpose, and the ability to make a meaningful contribution to society.

Adopting abundance rather than scarcity is a crucial component of this worldview. It entails realizing that there are countless chances available to those who are willing to look for them and that life is not a zero-sum game. This way of thinking encourages a can-do attitude rather than dwelling on limits and views problems as opportunities to grow rather than as hurdles to be avoided.

Dispelling Myths about Overnight Success

The temptation of sudden success frequently seduces young business people and those looking to get rich, but it's a lie that has to be dispelled. Success tales that appear to have occurred overnight sometimes conceal years of effort, hard work, learning, and perseverance. It is essential to dispel this myth since it promotes a more realistic viewpoint.

Overnight success is frequently a mirage, a highlight reel that leaves out the adversities experienced in secret. It's crucial to realize that reaching large riches or ambitions typically requires time, work, and patience. By accepting this truth, you may more effectively get ready for the voyage by establishing reasonable expectations and strengthening your will to keep going despite difficulties.

The Power of Mindset Shifts

Your attitude is a dynamic force that can be molded and sculpted; it is not a permanent attribute. The ability to change one's perspective is like discovering a secret superpower. It's about realizing that your ideas and convictions are flexible.

- **Growth Mindset:** It is a significant change to go from a fixed mindset to a growing attitude. Adopting a growth mindset is realizing that skills and intellect can be improved with commitment and effort. This change encourages resiliency, flexibility, and the capacity to take on problems.

5

- **Positive Self-Talk:** Your internal dialogue matters. Your perspective may be greatly altered by switching from self-criticism to self-encouragement. Confidence is increased, self-doubt is decreased, and a can-do attitude is promoted through positive self-talk.
- **Embracing Change:** Change is resisted by a rigid attitude but welcomed by a flexible mindset. Recognizing that change is a part of life and learning to accept it rather than dread it is where the power resides.

Setting Realistic Financial Goals

The checkpoints on your path to financial success are your goals. The key to success is setting reasonable financial objectives since they give your efforts focus and direction.

- **Clarity:** Clear, defined financial goals are indicative of realistic financial aspirations. They provide answers to the "what," "why," and "how" of your financial goals. Goals with little specificity are more difficult to achieve.
- **Measurability:** Objectives should be measurable. You ought to be able to monitor your development and recognize your successes. You can maintain your motivation and concentration thanks to this.
- **Achievability:** The key is realism. Ambitious objectives are wonderful, but they should also be feasible given your existing situation. Unattainable objectives can cause frustration and discouragement.
- **Time-Bound:** Without a deadline, a goal is only a desire. Setting a deadline encourages you to take regular action by

fostering a sense of urgency and accountability.

These ideas serve as the cornerstone of your path "From Aspirations to Achievement" in the realm of wealth thinking. You'll find yourself on a path toward not only financial success but also personal growth and fulfillment if you comprehend, accept, and apply them to your life.

3

BUILDING A STRONG FINANCIAL FOUNDATION

Your financial foundation is a core set of behaviors and routines that will help you achieve the long-term financial security and stability you need to plan, construct, and live the life you desire.

Money is more than just that. The power of money. Your ability to quit living paycheck to paycheck, eliminate debt, and begin accumulating money depends on having a solid financial foundation. It's what allows you the freedom to quit a terrible relationship, poor roommate, or bad job. It gives you courage to know that you have the means to stand up again if you fall. Instead of causing tension, it transforms money into a source of power.

Financial Literacy: A Cornerstone

Your financial future is founded on the often-overlooked but indisputable foundational skill of financial literacy. Understanding the fundamentals of money management, investments, and the complexities of the financial world are at the heart of financial literacy. It's the ability to make wise financial decisions, which is the exact definition of empowerment.

Understanding ideas like compound interest, inflation, and the numerous kinds of financial products accessible are all part of financial literacy. Making wise financial decisions becomes like attempting to navigate a maze while wearing blinders. Financial literacy teaches you to distinguish between good and bad debt, spot investment possibilities, and create plans to safeguard your financial future.

Budgeting for Success

Your financial achievement is mapped out in your budget. Your expenditure should be purposefully directed rather than being severely constrained. You can achieve your financial objectives and keep a healthy balance between spending and saving by creating a well-structured budget that ensures your financial resources are allocated effectively.

In order to create a budget, you must precisely document your income and spending. You can see where your money is going and pinpoint places where modifications may be made thanks to this. You may take charge of your financial life by classifying your costs and establishing restrictions.

Limiting discretionary spending is only one aspect of an effective budget; it also involves giving priority to saving and investing. It guarantees that you have the resources to achieve both your short-term and long-term goals, whether they include establishing a business, buying a home, or retiring comfortably.

Debt Management Strategies

Debt may have two sharp edges. It may be a tool for investment and progress when handled carefully. But if managed incorrectly, it may end up costing you money.

- **Understanding the difference between good and bad debt:** Not all debt is created equal. Knowing the difference between good and bad debt, such as a mortgage for a home or high-interest credit card debt, is made easier by financial literacy. You're advised to pay off high-interest loans in the order of priority.
- **Plans for Debt Reduction:** Having a good understanding of finances gives you the tools to reduce your debt. The avalanche approach and the snowball method, which prioritize paying off high-interest bills first, are two examples of how to do this.
- **Avoiding Accumulation:** Preventing debt accumulation is perhaps the most important component of managing debt. By promoting cautious credit use and discouraging impulsive expenditure, financial literacy helps prevent debt.

Saving and Emergency Funds

Your capacity to plan ahead for the unexpected will determine your financial security. Savings and emergency savings can be used in this situation. These savings serve as a safety net, shielding you from unforeseen costs and assisting you in getting through tough times without jeopardizing your long-term financial objectives.

Savings include both short- and long-term objectives. While long-term savings are set aside for retirement or sizable investments, short-term savings cover foreseeable costs like holidays or house maintenance. You may assure dependable contributions by automating your savings.

Contrarily, emergency funds are cash set aside in case of unanticipated events like sudden job loss, auto repairs, or medical issues. There should be enough money in these funds to pay for living costs for three to six months. You may avoid going into debt by having an emergency fund built up in case of unforeseen setbacks.

These elements—financial literacy, budgeting, debt management, and savings—are your building bricks in the process of laying a solid financial foundation. They equip you with the information, resources, and planning techniques required to build a solid and secure financial future.

4

INVESTING WISELY FOR LONG-TERM GROWTH

A deliberate approach to managing one's financial resources with the aim of obtaining sustained and significant returns over a prolonged time is investing intelligently for long-term growth. This strategy places a strong emphasis on the value of endurance, variety, and well-informed choices. Diversifying your investing portfolio over many asset classes, including equities, bonds, real estate, and even alternative assets like cryptocurrencies or commodities, is essential. By distributing the risk, diversification can reduce how much market volatility affects your overall profits. It's critical to match your investing decisions to your financial objectives, risk tolerance, and time horizon.

Keeping a long-term perspective also means restraining yourself from acting rashly in response to momentary market changes. Investors should avoid making emotionally motivated selections and instead concentrate on the underlying characteristics of the investments they have picked. Over time, regular investments into your portfolio, such as those made through dollar-cost averaging, can help you profit from market volatility. By utilizing the force of compounding, this strategy enables your investments to increase continuously over time.

Additionally, intelligent investment for long-term prosperity necessitates continual education and keeping up with market and economic developments. To keep your chosen asset allocation, you must regularly examine and rebalance your portfolio as necessary. Finally, it's critical to seek the advice of financial experts or advisers who can direct you and assist you in creating a thorough investment strategy customized to your specific financial circumstances and long-term objectives. Investors may increase their prospects of long-term wealth accumulation and risk management by adhering to these guidelines and keeping a disciplined attitude.

Principles of Successful Investing

A set of timeless principles serve as the foundation for successful investing, which is a disciplined craft. The rule of doing your homework and exercising due diligence comes first. It is crucial to fully comprehend what you are investing in before you put your hard-earned money into it. This entails investigating a company's financial stability, competitive land-scape, and expansion opportunities. It also entails remaining knowledgeable about world events and economic trends that might affect your finances.

The need of having a well-thought-out investing strategy is another essential idea. This plan should be in line with your financial objectives, level of risk tolerance, and time frame.

Are you making investments to fund retirement, a down payment on a property, or long-term wealth accumulation? Your investing plan should take these goals into account.

Finally, discipline and patience are required for effective investing. Markets may be erratic, and gyrations in price are unavoidable. Decisions based on emotion are frequently unsuccessful. Your chances of long-term success rise when you stick to a well laid out investing strategy and resist the impulse to move rashly in response to market volatility.

Diversification and Risk Management

A tried-and-true method for reducing risk in your financial portfolio is diversification. It entails distributing your investments across several businesses, geographies, and asset classes. The objective is to lessen the effect of subpar performance in any one investment or industry on your portfolio as a whole.

By diversifying, you reduce the chance that a market downturn may cause you to lose a sizable amount of your investment. Diversification helps to make sure that your portfolio is resilient in the face of market volatility, even while it does not completely remove risk.

Knowing your risk tolerance is another important aspect of risk management. What level of comfort do you have with the prospect of losing all or part of your investment? This evaluation guides your asset allocation and investing decisions. It's critical to create a balance that's in line with your risk tolerance because investments with larger potential returns sometimes also include higher degrees of risk.

Exploring Investment Vehicles

Numerous investment vehicles are available, each with a unique risk-return profile. Stocks, bonds, property, mutual funds, exchange-traded funds (ETFs), and other choices are typical. Your financial objectives and risk tolerance will determine the type of investment vehicle you use.

- **Stocks** represent ownership in a company and offer the potential for significant capital appreciation. They are more volatile than other investments but can yield substantial returns over the long term.
- **Bonds** are debt securities issued by governments or corporations. They provide regular interest payments and are generally considered less risky than stocks. Bonds are often used to provide income and stability in a portfolio.
- **Real Estate** offers the opportunity to invest in physical assets like residential or commercial properties. Real estate investments can provide rental income and the potential for property appreciation.
- **Mutual Funds** pool money from multiple investors to invest in a diversified portfolio of stocks, bonds, or other securities. They are managed by professional fund managers and offer diversification and professional management.
- **ETFs** are similar to mutual funds but trade like stocks on exchanges. They offer diversification, liquidity, and often lower fees than mutual funds.

Patience: The Investor's Virtue

Patience is arguably the most important quality for investors.

15

Short-term market changes are an element of successful investing's long-term path. It's essential to fight the impulse to impulsively acquire and sell investments based on passing trends or feelings.

You can withstand market downturns and gain from the power of compounding over time by being patient. Your investment potential increases the longer you keep it in the market. Markets often bounce back after downturns, according to history, and persistent investors often profit.

5

ENTREPRENEURIAL MINDSET

A collection of attitudes, actions, and cognitive patterns known as an entrepreneurial mentality allow people to recognize and exploit chances to build revenue streams. Strong sense of initiative, a readiness to accept calculated risks, and a persistent desire for innovation and problem-solving are characteristics of it. People with an entrepreneurial attitude are never satisfied with the status quo and are always searching for new sources of income outside of the regular nine-to-five work.

The entrepreneurial mindset places a strong emphasis on generating revenue sources. People with this mentality aggressively seek out and build several revenue sources as opposed to merely depending on one source of income. Beginning a side company, investing in stocks or real estate, freelancing, or generating passive income streams like royalties or licensing agreements are a few examples of how to diversify your income. Other options include beginning a side business. A variety of income sources that can offer financial stability and flexibility, lower risk, and eventually result in financial independence are desired.

In essence, the entrepreneurial mentality equips people—even those who aren't typical entrepreneurs—to think like company owners. It motivates people to actively seek out possibilities, adjust to shifting conditions, and never stop learning and developing. People may improve their financial security and follow their hobbies and ambitions with more freedom and assurance by adopting this mentality and working aggressively to generate revenue streams.

The Entrepreneurial Spirit

A special combination of traits, such as inventiveness, resiliency, tenacity, and a constant search of possibilities, define the entrepreneurial spirit. It's about tackling issues with a problem-solving mindset and viewing obstacles as opportunities. This mentality is frequently motivated by a strong desire to realize ideas, provide value, and take calculated risks.

Entrepreneurs have a natural capacity to predict the future, identifying trends and market gaps that others might miss. They are continuously looking for methods to enhance current goods or services or create completely new ones, and they thrive on innovation. A desire for independence, a readiness to accept uncertainty, and the confidence to carve one's own path in the commercial world are at the heart of the entrepreneurial spirit.

Identifying Profitable Opportunities

The lifeblood of entrepreneurship is the discovery of lucrative possibilities. It requires careful market analysis, a thorough comprehension of consumer requirements, and the capacity to recognize patterns that point to possible development areas. Successful business people are adept at seeing market gaps, unmet demands, or situations where they can provide a special solution.

A key step in this procedure is market research. It aids business owners in data collection, understanding consumer behavior, and competitive analysis. With this information at hand, they may create goods or services that cater to certain needs or offer creative fixes.

Additionally, seeing lucrative chances calls for the capacity to adjust and pivot as required. The business environment is continuously changing, and successful businesspeople are adaptable enough to change their offers and tactics to stay current and satisfy shifting customer expectations.

Launching and Scaling Your Business

The beginning of a firm is a crucial phase for entrepreneurs. It include putting concepts into practice, launching goods or services, and creating a brand identity. Planning thoroughly, allocating resources, and being aware of market trends are all necessary.

Successful businesspeople frequently start off small and expand gradually. A minimum viable product (MVP) may be used as a starting point to gauge interest and obtain feedback. They expand their commercial activities to serve a wider clientele and satisfy rising demand as they acquire traction and confidence.

Expanding product lines, breaking into new markets, or diversifying income streams are all examples of strategic decisions that must be made while scaling a corporation. To successfully assist development, entrepreneurs must also take into account elements like funding, team building, and operational efficiency.

Managing Entrepreneurial Risks

There are dangers involved with becoming an entrepreneur, and risk management is a crucial part of the process. Unmanaged risks, however, can result in failure or setbacks while well controlled risks can yield significant returns. Entrepreneurs need to take a proactive approach to risk management.

The first step in risk management is to identify possible hazards. Market risks, financial risks, operational risks, and legal risks are all included in this. Entrepreneurs must evaluate the possibility of these risks occurring and their possible effects on their company.

Entrepreneurs can create risk reduction measures once the risks have been recognized. This can entail diversifying your sources of income, making backup plans, getting insurance, or hiring a lawyer to be sure you're following the law.

The entrepreneurial attitude is a powerful force that motivates people to spot lucrative possibilities, start and grow enterprises, and efficiently handle risks. It's a way of thinking that is based on creativity, innovation, and an unshakable commitment to adding value and improving the world. Entrepreneurs are the driving forces behind economic expansion, and their zeal and tenacity continue to mold the commercial environment.

6

NAVIGATING CHALLENGES AND FAILURES

Any route towards achievement always involves navigating obstacles and setbacks. When faced with difficulty, it's essential to view these challenges as priceless teaching moments rather than impassable barriers. Overcoming these obstacles may be made much easier by adopting a growth mindset, which entails viewing failures as stepping stones to advancement. One can develop resilience, flexibility, and determination by accepting that failures are a normal part of any attempt. Additionally, it's crucial to remain committed to long-term objectives and keep an optimistic outlook since these traits may support motivation and drive during challenging circumstances.

Failures, no matter how big or little, can offer priceless insights into what went wrong and how to fix it. People might focus their efforts into a useful post-mortem analysis instead of wallowing on disappointment. This entails analyzing the underlying reasons for the failure, finding potential improvement areas, and coming up with a strategy to address these flaws. Additionally, getting advice from peers or mentors who have dealt with comparable difficulties might provide new insights and pointers on the way forward. Accepting setbacks as a necessary part of the success process might ultimately result in greater skill development and personal development.

Maintaining perspective and keeping the greater picture in mind are crucial in the face of difficulty. Even though they might be demoralizing in the moment, difficulties and failures frequently help build a solid foundation for success in the future. Effectively overcoming these challenges requires resilience, adaptation, and a dedication to ongoing growth. In essence, the road to success is not a straight one but rather a twisting one with highs and lows. Individuals may grow more capable, self-assured, and ultimately more prepared to accomplish their goals by accepting difficulties and learning from setbacks.

The Role of Resilience

The foundation upon which successful business people and people manage difficulties and setbacks is resilience. It is the capacity to overcome obstacles and keep going forward with tenacity after experiencing failures. Being resilient is a talent that may be developed over time; it is not an intrinsic feature.

Individuals that are resilient demonstrate emotional fortitude in the face of difficulty. They recognise their feelings, whether they be anger, sadness, or even fear, but they do not allow these feelings to keep them from acting. Instead, they utilize them as motivation to keep pushing through challenges.

Maintaining a growth mindset—the conviction that setbacks are chances for development and learning—is another aspect of resilience. It's about seeing obstacles as transitory setbacks that can be overcome rather than insurmountable obstacles. Setbacks simply serve to redouble the resolve of those who are resilient in their pursuit of their objectives.

Learning from Setbacks

Failures do not result from setbacks; rather, they serve as lessons. Every obstacle that is faced along the way to success is an opportunity for learning and development. Successful people are aware of this underlying reality and view failure as an opportunity to grow.

The initial response to a setback is to perform a post-mortem investigation. What happened? What may have been done otherwise? What may be learned from the situation? People can get important insights that can guide their decisions and actions in the future by asking these questions.

Humility—the readiness to acknowledge when errors have been made—is another necessary quality for learning from failures. It's about realizing that nobody is perfect and that even the most accomplished people have encountered obstacles along the way. Adversity may be a stimulus for both personal and professional development if one adopts a growth attitude and learns from failures.

Overcoming Fear of Failure

A significant roadblock that can impede development and discourage innovation is fear of failure. The crippling conviction that failure is disastrous and irreparable. But successful people have a different perspective on failure. They perceive it as a crucial stop along the road to success—a essential intermediate stage.

Reframing one's connection with failure is necessary to overcome the fear of failure. It's important to realize that failure is not a measure of one's value or potential. It is basically feedback, indicating that changes or advancements are required. When failure is viewed in this way, people are less afraid of it and are more eager to take measured chances and rise to new challenges.

In addition, people who get over their fear of failing frequently develop a compassionate attitude toward themselves. They are polite and understanding toward themselves, just as they would be to a buddy going through a similar scenario. This self-compassion fosters an environment of inner acceptance that supports resilience and tenacity.

Turning Obstacles into Stepping Stones

Even the most difficult obstacles can act as helpful stepping stones on the way to achievement. Successful people understand that challenges aren't insurmountable hurdles, but rather chances for development and creativity. They tackle challenges with a mindset for solving problems and a dedication to doing so.

People frequently use inventiveness and creativity to convert challenges into stepping stones. To get around obstacles, they look for alternate paths, take into account various strategies, and make use of their network and resources. They success-fully overcome the challenge while learning new abilities and information that will help them in the future.

Additionally, keeping a long-term perspective is necessary for converting challenges into stepping stones. It is the knowledge that one's overarching trajectory is not defined by temporary setbacks. Instead, each challenge faced advances people closer to their ultimate objectives and aspirations while bolstering their resiliency and resolve along the way.

In conclusion, overcoming obstacles and failing is a crucial component of any path to success. The qualities of people who not only weather the storms but come out stronger and more competent on the other side include resilience, the capacity to learn from failures, fortitude to face failure head-on, and the ability to convert hurdles into stepping stones. Success is the capacity to overcome obstacles, not their absence.

7

CULTIVATING ABUNDANCE
BEYOND MONEY

Balancing Wealth with Well-being
Genuine wealth extends beyond material possessions and encompasses overall well being which comprises physical and emotional health. Striking a balance between prosperity and wealth is crucial for leading a purposeful existence. It's important to recognize that no amount of achievement is worth compromising one's well being and happiness.

Achieving harmony between prosperity and wealth necessitates making choices about self care. This entails maintaining a lifestyle through exercise, a nutritious diet and sufficient rest. Taking care of one's emotional well being also involves practicing mindfulness, managing stress effectively and seeking assistance when required. Ultimately prioritizing happiness plays a role in attaining success. When individuals prioritize their health and happiness they are better able to savor the rewards of accomplishments while living gratifying lives.

Building Healthy Relationships

From a wider perspective, wealth encompasses the strength of our social bonds. Good connections form part of an authentic, wealthy existence. Ties that span friendships, families, workmates, and society at large are all included here.

Building a harmonious partnership depends on the cornerstones of mutual understanding and reliance. Through them, one finds happiness and completion, accompanied by emotional backing and a feeling of connection. Developing strong bonds with others demands genuine interest and consistent investment of effort, compassion, plus persistence.

Giving and getting are part of relationship wealth that also comprises both. Acts of charitable behavior are the cornerstone of meaningful ties.

Finding Fulfillment Beyond Material Success

While important, accomplishing financial goals will not automatically lead to joy. Wherever one discovers their passion and reason, therein lies true fulfillment. Fulfillment depends on aligning personal beliefs with societal expectations and active engagement.

Contentment requires exploring oneself; money alone cannot buy happiness. To determine your path forward, you must first discover your underlying ideals. Personal growth necessitates leaving your comfort zone behind and taking on new problems and possibilities.

Achievements and successes contribute significantly to feelings of contentment, adding to overall satisfaction. One's passion and value alignment can result in heightened satisfaction and a greater sense of purpose.

The Wealth of Contribution in Giving Back

While financial success may seem like an important measure, giving back holds much more weight when discussing long-term wealth accumulation. Contributions come in the form of gifts which benefit both the giver and receiver equally. Time and effort put into benefiting those around you and your broader community is necessary when contributing to their betterment.

Giving back encompasses a range of actions, such as mentoring, donating time/money, & pursuing causes aligned w/personal beliefs. Giving fosters societal progress by fortifying community foundations while simultaneously deepening interpersonal ties.

Financial value isn't all; contributions hold more significance than meets the eye. This category covers the distribution of educational material, including wisdom and personal anecdotes. Those who donate their time and resources experience a profound feeling of abundance that transcends monetary gain.

Beyond purely economic growth lies the full scope of abundant qualities including meaningful labor, positive social ties, enjoyment, and holistic flourishing. To grasp the full scope of wellbeing, one must acknowledge that material affluence merges with a life defined by direction and significance. Life's true richness unfolds when these components are equally prioritized.

8

HOW TO KEEP THE MILLIONAIRE MINDSET

The Ongoing Journey
A millionaire mentality requires ongoing effort rather than a final goal. Financial success calls for persistent hard work and steadfast determination. Awareness of this truth can motivate lifelong advancement, meaningful contributions, and lasting value creation.

Early achievement opens up further objectives, rather than signaling conclusion; continued effort follows suit. Breaking new grounds has become crucial to achieving goals, so keep pushing limits! Material wealth takes a back seat when pursuing fresh objectives and dreams because doing so typically imbues fulfillment and meaning into the lives of those who succeed.

Staying Informed and Adapting
Being knowledgeable and flexible allows one to sustain a millionaire perspective amidst rapid change. Change in finan-

cial marketplaces, businesses, and technologies necessitates continuous adaptation; failure to comply may leave you in the dust. Awareness and continuous learning are essential qualities found among prosperous individuals.

Part of maintaining awareness, one must keep pace with evolving market conditions. To gain ground, one must invest their time in education and seek new learning. Professionally minded individuals maintain their status by consistently participating in book reading, conventions, and interpersonal interactions.

Flexibility is also essential. Being open to change and willing to adapt is crucial. Success hinges upon adaptability; deviate when needed.

Cultivating a Growth Mindset

A growth mindset is crucial when striving toward a millionaire status. Enhancing one's aptitudes and IQ requires unwavering commitment and diligent practice. Growth mindset individuals consider difficulties as opportunities; they view failures as lessons learned via this lens.

Two critical components of fostering a growth mindset include testing limits and wholeheartedly tackling challenges. To achieve success later on, one must view past failures as stepping stones. Persisting amidst hardships requires individuals who embrace growth to seek ways to enhance themselves and their objectives constantly.

Being around like-minded individuals offers support and

encouragement to those pursuing goals similar to yours, which can lead to increased motivation and self-assurance.

Mentorship and Legacy in Paying It Forward

To think like a millionaire, paying it forward is essential. Mentoring plays an important role in fostering individual growth across both personal and professional realms. Through mentoring partnerships, successful individuals search for experienced mentors offering wise counsel, insight, and expertise gained via personal journeying.

Two individuals stand to gain when they engage in mentoring; hence it is a two-way street. Aiding people in realizing their objectives brings joy to those who act as role models because they also contribute to shaping the following generation. By means of mentoring, mentees receive beneficial guidance, reassurance, and connections.

Having a prosperous mindset demands considering one's legacy... Supporting initiatives consistent with your beliefs and interests forms part of leaving a lasting legacy. By posing queries about leaving a lasting imprint on the planet, we examine how our financial resources and intellectual prowess might positively influence society.

Maintaining a wealthy mindset requires constant learning, versatility, openness to development, and contributing back to society; these elements form the cornerstone of this mental attitude throughout one's life. Unlocking monetary prosperity requires recognizing how different elements contribute to an entire life filled with significance. Following these precepts enables individuals to advance, thrive, & leave a lasting legacy throughout their lives.

9

CONCLUSION

I n the grand finale of our journey, we arrive not at an end, but at a beginning—a new chapter in your life, one where aspirations become achievements, and dreams transform into reality. "From Aspirations to Achievement: Nurturing Your Millionaire Mindset" has been your guide, your mentor, and your steadfast companion in the pursuit of financial abundance and personal growth.

Throughout these pages, we've explored the intricacies of the millionaire mindset, revealing the keys to its nurturing and the wisdom it imparts. We've touched upon the principles of financial literacy, the art of investing wisely, and the spirit of entrepreneurship. We've also journeyed into the depths of your psyche, examining the beliefs and behaviors that shape your relationship with money.

But beyond the knowledge imparted, this book has aimed to inspire a fundamental shift within you—a shift toward empowered action, unwavering determination, and an unshakable belief in your own potential. You now understand that the path to prosperity is not paved with shortcuts or overnight successes, but with consistent effort, resilience in the face of setbacks, and the courage to chase your dreams even when they seem distant.

As we close this chapter, remember that the journey toward a millionaire mindset is ongoing. It's a journey that transcends financial wealth and enters the realm of personal fulfillment, resilience, and a deep sense of purpose. It's about using your newfound knowledge to not only enhance your life but also to impact the lives of others positively.

Now, armed with the tools, strategies, and wisdom gained from this exploration, you have the power to forge a future that aligns with your aspirations. Your journey may take unexpected turns, and there will be challenges to overcome, but your mindset is now your greatest asset—a guiding star illuminating the path to your dreams.

In closing, embrace your journey with enthusiasm and courage. Nurture your millionaire mindset, for it's not just about becoming wealthy; it's about becoming the best version of yourself. Remember that success, in all its forms, is a journey, not a destination. Aspire, act, achieve, and repeat—the cycle of growth that knows no bounds.

Your millionaire mindset is not a final achievement; it's a lifelong companion. So, my fellow traveler, go forth with confidence, audacity, and the unwavering belief that the best is yet to come. Your aspirations have met their match in your determination, and the achievements waiting for you are as boundless as your dreams.

www.ingramcontent.com/pod-product-compliance
Lightning Source LLC
Chambersburg PA
CBHW072221290526
45794CB00007B/2842